C000172996

797,885 Books

are available to read at

www.ForgottenBooks.com

Forgotten Books' App
Available for mobile, tablet & eReader

ISBN 978-1-333-07085-4
PIBN 10462721

1 MONTH OF
FREE
READING

at
www.ForgottenBooks.com

By purchasing this book you are
eligible for one month membership to
ForgottenBooks.com, giving you
unlimited access to our entire
collection of over 700,000 titles via
our web site and mobile apps.

To claim your free month visit:

www.forgottenbooks.com/free462721

English
Français
Deutsche
Italiano
Español
Português

www.forgottenbooks.com

Mythology Photography **Fiction**
Fishing Christianity **Art** Cooking
Essays Buddhism Freemasonry
Medicine **Biology** Music **Ancient
Egypt** Evolution Carpentry Physics
Dance Geology **Mathematics** Fitness
Shakespeare **Folklore** Yoga Marketing
Confidence Immortality Biographies
Poetry **Psychology** Witchcraft
Electronics Chemistry History **Law**
Accounting **Philosophy** Anthropology
Alchemy Drama Quantum Mechanics
Atheism Sexual Health **Ancient History**
Entrepreneurship Languages Sport
Paleontology Needlework Islam
Metaphysics Investment Archaeology
Parenting Statistics Criminology
Motivational

LILIAN MAY.

HARRISBURG, PENN'A.

M DCCC LII.

CONTENTS.

POEMS.

PROEM.

Lone wand'ring on the shore of Life's vast ocean,
    A voice, low murm'ring, came upon the tide,
Unto my spirit, longing in its heart devotion—
    As mem'ries of the Past have come and died.

There came to me across the wave-strand Real,
    A beauteous image of a bright-eyed one—
The semblance of my boy-hood's loved Ideal—
    As glories over Dream-Land loves are thrown.

And when I caught her sight the more than vision
    Entranced me with the magic of her song,—
Melodious minstrel-lays from climes elysian
    Were borne upon the Summer breeze along.

As down upon the waters noon-day shimmered
    In molten-glows of gorgeous Summer sheen,
And June-rays beaming, brightly glimmered,
    Her blue eye glisten'd purely fair, I ween.

I watched her as the golden sun-light faded
   From off the em'rald brow of weary earth,
As cherish'd haunts of Summer-time were shaded,
   And cottagers were gath'ring 'round the hearth.

The eve-stars hung aloft o'er wild and Prairie,
   As in their glorious gyres they joyous swung,
And thro' the ruins old, deserted, airy,
   The sweet sound of a loved Æolian rung.

'T was then there came a joyous radiant maiden,
   As the meek star-light gleam'd o'er hill and le
And sat her by my side, the weary-laden,
   And softly whisper'd all her love to me.

Now ev'ry eve, when silvery moon-beams brighten
   And throw a halo o'er my childhood's home,
When wild-stars field and greenwood lighten,
   Those lovely visions of my Ideal come.

And here, my friends, ye have the songs she chanted
   In dreary Winter, Summer-time and Spring,—
Of the bright days when she my boy-home haunted
   Mementos, cherish'd—ah, too well!—I bring.

ELLIE.

A SPRING-TIME LAY.

The Winter that linger'd so long, Ellie,
   Hath fled to his home away,
Hath gone on the breath of the wind, Ellie,
   On the blast of the April day;
The maiden Spring is blithe, Ellie,
   Tho' coy as a fair young bride,
Yet she came to our childhood's home, Ellie,
   In the joy of the bright May-tide.

Over the vales and the hills, Ellie,
   And the forest dells she 's been;
And down by the gurgling streams, Ellie,
   Her pathway is covered with green;
O, down in the wild-wood glen, Ellie,
   Was ever such music heard,
As the matin-hymn in the morn, Ellie,
   Of the early Spring-time bird?

2

The honey-bee wingeth his way, Ellie,
 O'er garden, and grove, and lawn,
Ere the day-god rouseth from sleep, Ellie,
 In the glorious blush of dawn;
O, dear is his hum in the dell, Ellie,
 Where blow the fair blossoms of May,
And gathereth sweets untold, Ellie,
 As the breeze with the flowers play.

O, what are the joys of life, Ellie,
 Without the smile of the flowers;
Can you not say that this, Ellie,
 Is a beautiful world of ours!
My soul is enraptured, Ellie, Ellie,
 As I hear the bright birds sing,
And heart-thanks go up to Him, Ellie,
 Who giveth his children Spring.

EARTH-FADING.

THE wild-wood darlings are dying, Ellie,
   That blossom'd in the May,
And the buds of beauty now blowing, Ellie,
   Are fading—"passing away;"
For the scorching glare of the Summer, Ellie,
   Hath blasted the little flowers,
Which the fairies in the Spring, Ellie,
   Brought from their South-Land bowers.

I thought that the Autumn alone, Ellie,
   A deadening blight would bring,
But I see the heat of Summer, Ellie,
   Hath wither'd the gems of Spring;
So the beautiful things of earth, Ellie,
   In their glow and their pride must die,
And the loved and cherished too well, Ellie,
   The first in the grave must lie.

The hectic flush on thy cheeks, Ellie,
  With its fearful, forboding hue,
And the pallid touch on thy brow, Ellie,
  Tells thou art passing too;—
Thou art passing away in thy pride, Ellie,
  In the glow of thy blooming youth,
In thy love and thy beauty divine, Ellie,
  And thy fond, unsullied truth.

When my "Ideal" wandered afar, Ellie,
  Thou still linger'd by my side;
And I hop'd ere the Summer would pass, Ellie,
  To claim thee my own—my bride!
But the chill of the Northern clime, Ellie,
  With the withering power of Death,
Is loitering now on the sill, Ellie,
  Ere it comes with *his* blighting breath.

I knew that the flowers of Spring, Ellie,
  'Fore the Autumn blast would fade,
That all the joys of the heart, Ellie,
  With sorrow were deep inlaid;
But I little thought in the May, Ellie,
  So soon the Destroyer would come,
And cut *thee* down in thy youth, Ellie,
  Thou pride of our hearth and home!

Now the June roses blow in the garden, Ellie,
   Close to the Southern wall,
And eve-stars shimmer adown, Ellie,
   A holied, pure light o'er all,—
And thou 'rt passing away in thy pride, Ellie,
   In the glow of thy blooming youth,
In thy love and thy beauty divine, Ellie,
   And thy fond, unsullied truth.

My eyes were dimming last night, Ellie—
   My heart is saddening still—
As I gazed on my bright heart-love, Ellie,
   O'er my frame came a shuddering chill,
For I saw that the silver chain, Ellie,
   Soon link from link would part,
That the golden bowl would break, Ellie,
   With the tablet of the heart.

And I laid me down on my couch, Ellie,
   And sued for the maiden sleep,
When I prayed to the Holy One, Ellie,
   His angel-watch to keep;
Tears filled my eyes as I sank, Ellie,
   To the Isles in the Land of Dreams,
Where toiling and striving ne'er come, Ellie,
   But LOVE with its joy-light teems.

I sat me down in the shade, Ellie,
  Near the shores of the sounding sea,
And thou wert there in thy love, Ellie,
  With my Ideal's minstrelsy;—
O, the words which thou whispered there, Ellie,
  Were the loves of a gentle heart,
In which the smiles of this world, Ellie,
  Could never, no never have part.

But the bands of the mystic spell, Ellie,
  Were sundered far too soon,
For the day-god gleam'd thro' the pane, Ellie,
  In the blush of the rosy June;
And as I awoke, a smile, Ellie,
  Seem'd resting upon thy face,—
Deep, deep in my heart lies mirror'd, Ellie,
  That dawn o'er our trysting-place.

Oh, the Real, cold and stark, Ellie,
  And its joys with sorrow e'er rife,
Came o'er the wake of my spell, Ellie,
  And shadow'd our Dream-Land Life;
Now the tears gather full in my eyes, Ellie,
  As I think of my early love,
Who is passing away from the earth, Ellie,
  To a glorious home above,

Where the angels sing forever, Ellie,
    And play on harps of gold;
Where all the glories eternal, Ellie,
    Soon, soon, thou shalt behold,—
Oh, thou 'rt passing away in thy pride, Ellie,
    In the glow of thy blooming youth,
In thy love and thy beauty divine, Ellie,
    And thy fond, unsullied truth.

Oh, my heart is sinking with wo, Ellie,
    For I know ere the roses have flown
Thou wilt go far away to Him, Ellie,
    Up, up to the Holy One's throne;—
His arm will strengthen thee then, Ellie,
    Thro' the dark and shadowy vale,
To whom thou 'st committed thy all, Ellie,—
    Thy trust shall never thee fail.

I cannot tarry behind, Ellie,
    I cannot wander here long,
For my soul must go with its love, Ellie,
    To swell the eternal song.
I would fain lie first in the grave, Ellie,
    Neath the shade of the willow tree,
Where the South-breeze requiems low, Ellie,
    And North-winds mournfully.

My heart will go down in the tomb, Ellie,
   With the heart of .my early love,
'Till our spirits shall meet afar, Ellie,
   In our Father's house above;
But why murmur I at His will, Ellie,
   At the will of the Holy One,
Who will take thee away to Himself, Ellie,
   By the side of the star-gemm'd throne.

I will try to live on in the world, Ellie,
   To buffet its every ill,
Alone its dark waves to withstand, Ellie,—
   Ay, *live for thy memory* still,—
Thou art passing away from earth, Ellie,
   In the glow of thy blooming youth,
In thy love and thy beauty divine, Ellie,
   And thy fond, unsullied truth.

LOVE-LOST.

They have lain thee down in the tomb, Ellie,
   Near by the willow-shade,
Where the birds in the early spring, Ellie,
   Their downy nest-homes made;—
The dark was o'er all when thou wander'dst, Ellie,
   Afar from the cottage wall,
To answer the summons which came, Ellie,—
   To answer the angel's call.

The hearth-stone is desolate now, Ellie,
   And vacant the study-chair;
We look in vain for the form, Ellie,
   That lingered so often there.
Oh, heavy the grief and the wo, Ellie,
   That holdeth in thrall my heart;—
Thy love and thy tenderness true, Ellie,
   Can never—no, never depart!

The cold sod is wet with the dew, Ellie,
   That the even hath brought from away,
And the flowers are wither'd and pale, Ellie,
   Which we strewed o'er thy grave to-day;
We scattered the roses of Summer, Ellie,
   In thy grave so cheerless and cold;—
But thou 'rt culling far fairer than they, Ellie,
   Away in the gardens of gold.

The watchers are pale to-night, Ellie,
   A sorrowful vigil they keep;
Yet the kiss of the wind is sweet, Ellie,
   As it husheth the flowers to sleep;
"Down into the tomb the loved, Ellie,
   Are ever the first to go,"
So mournful I sang when the roses, Ellie,
   By cottage and hamlet did blow.

They chanted a dirge o'er thy grave, Ellie,
   —A requiem soft and low,
But the tones were too sad for my heart, Ellie,
   And I sank 'neath the weight of my wo;
They gather'd me up from thy grave, Ellie,
   And bore me away, away,
That I might not see where my love, Ellie,
   In her beauty divine did lay.

The end of this strife will come, Ellie,
    When our Father seeth best,
And take me afar to Himself, Ellie,
    Where the weary at last will rest;
How gladly I'll hasten to thee, Ellie,
    Near the shores of the mighty sea,
Where I shall behold thee forever, Ellie,—
    My love and my life, Ellie!

THE MAIDEN OF MY HEART.

FAR away in my childhood's home,
  In the land of the spreading vine,
Sings a maiden fair, with auburn hair,
  Like the birds in the Summer-time.

And I love the songs the maiden sings,
  Away in the lonely wood,
In the morning's blush and the evening's hush,
  To the sound of the roaring flood.

Over her pale brow the dark tresses fall—
  A goddess of beauty and love—
The light of her eyes like stars in the skies,
  Beameth on me from above.

By a magic spell my heart is caught,
  With the songs she sings of yore;
And over my soul now the sad strains roll,
  As the dirge for a lost " Lenore."

The maiden with power entrancing hath held,
  My spirit hath tried to enchain ;
Like a blissful light o'er my darkening night,
  From afar cometh on the strain.

And oft in the midnight dim and dark,
  As in the forests of eld,
Comes the murmuring sound, in the ether round,
  That often my spirit hath held.

Now over the strings of my trembling lyre
  The maiden her fingers run ;
Such the mintrelsy she harpeth to me,
  I sigh when the singer's done.

IN MEMORIAM.

Thou art gone, the loved and loving one, in thy early manhood's
      prime,
While the flush of youth was bright and warm, in Life's gay
      Summer-time ;
I ne'er may grasp thy friendly hand, nor meet thy warm embrace :
I ne'er may see thy smiling eye, nor greet thy welcome face ;
Life's roseate hues hath fled and left a pure but pallid brow—
And thou, my friend, the true and tried, oh ! tell me where art
      thou ?

Alas ! thou 'rt gone, from earth away, to the shadows of the dead !
They have ta'en thee to thy slumber—earth's pillow for thy
      head ;
Thou hast gone, and gone forever, the stateliest of the band—
Thou hast passed, and passed forever, unto the Spirit-land ;
Earth's fondest and its brightest hopes on fleeting pinions fly,
And the soul-loved and cherished buds are ever the first to die !

And thou, the dearest and the best, oh, brother, friend and son !
Earth's joys and cares have fled apace—thy life's last sands hath
    run !
And thou, the good and pure of heart, with Faith's bright beam-
    ing eye,
Hath crossed unto the far-off shores of the dread Eternity ;
Tho' thou hast gone, yet memory chants a wild impassioned lay,
Of one who loved and was beloved in his early childhood's day ;

Thou are resting calmly, Vincent, beneath Indiana's sod,—
Thro' the pathway of the dim and silent valley thou hast trod ;
The Summer breeze is singing 'round thy grave a solemn dirge—
Softly floats its music o'er thy own White's gentle surge ;—
Sorrow hath o'er my stricken heart now thrown its wayward spell ;
Adieu, thou early loved and lost ! lamented friend, farewell.

AN AUTUMN EVENING.

Now a hallowed stillness reigneth
  Over thicket, hill and dale,
Save the music of the streamlet
  As it murmurs thro' the vale.
All are hushed to rest and quiet
  In the mellow even-tide,
For the forest-flowers are dying—
  Fading is the Summer's pride.

Forest leaves are growing yellow
  As stern Winter draweth nigh,
When the Frost-King, cold and icy,
  On the night-wind rideth high ;
And the golden glow of even
  Feels the shadow of the night,
Like a halo o'er our spirits
  Gleam the starry gems of light !

TO SPRING.

" I marked the Spring as she passed along,
With her eye of light and her lip of song!"—W. G. CLARKE.

HAIL, genial Spring ! I've waited long
    To feel thy breath upon my brow ;
Thou 'st come with love, and joy, and song,—
    A happy welcome to thee now !

And o'er the wreck that Winter's made
    A kindly pall thou e'er dost fling ;
And all his power, his pomp, parade,
    Hath vanish'd in thy smiles, O, Spring !

Welcome ! I hear the warbling birds—
    Their notes my aching heart doth fill ;
O, welcome ! the unfettered herds
    Are playing on the flowery hill.

I've found the violet and the rose
    Which wither'd 'fore the Autumn blast;—
The lily from its soft repose,
    So fresh and pure, I've plucked at last.

Thou hast again the rills set free,—
    I love to hear their music rare;
While blooming is each forest tree
    That yields its perfume to the air.

The grass is green which waveth o'er
    A loved mother's humble tomb,
The birds of Spring their matins pour
    Above her dark and cheerless home.

And flowers in wild luxuriance grow
    Above the grave-yard's hallow'd spot,
Where Winter's wind and Winter's snow
    Of late moan'd forth *earth's common lot!*

And of the blitheful Summer, Spring,
    A faithful monitor art thou,
For Summer ripens what thou dost bring,
    And what thou 'rt giving birth to now.

Thus, like the morning of our life,
  And the bright sunshine of our day,
Art thou, O, Spring, with pleasures rife,
  'Til youth itself doth fade away!

Then hail thee, Spring! I've waited long
  To feel thy breath upon my brow;
Thou'st come with love, and life, and song—
  A happy welcome to thee now!

LINES ON LEAVING HOME.

Oh, fare thee well, my early childhood's home !
   A shade of sadness cometh o'er my brow,
   As with a heavy heart I leave thee now,
'Mid other scenes of gloom or joy to roam.

Oh, fare thee well ! loved scenes of early years
   Come with the mem'ries of the happy Past—
   Come to my heart, and o'er its joy doth cast
A pensive sorrow of out-gushing tears.

Now come the thoughts of joyous boyhood's hours—
   The shadow mingling with the sun's bright beam—
   The fond hopes of a youthful poet's dream—
Life's gladsome Spring-time wreath'd with fairest flowers.

Thou, too, my Susquehanna, dearly-loved!
    Memory to mind shall often bring the while
    Thy bright-blue waters and each gorgeous isle;—
We part; I cannot go with heart unmoved.

Tho' I turn my steps from my native home,
    O, never shall forgetfulness o'ercast
    And loose the bonds affection holdeth fast—
Should ocean divide us, and far I roam.

Farewell! I go—'t is with a tearful eye,
    And my lips falter, aye my heart is sad;
    I leave thee; farewell! I am aught but glad,—
I go with a love that never can die.

LIFE.

Life is like the Summer flower
  That boweth to the breeze,
In its mild and sunniest hour,
Wafting by its futile power
  The sweets to far-off seas;—
Fading, when the sultry noon
Of the bright, unclouded June
Comes with hot and scorching breath,
And the blasting flame of Death.

Life is like the season's Spring
  That comes with song and glee;—
Thought flies upward on the wing,
Bidding nature with her sing
  Heaven's rapt'rous minstrelsy;
Yet Spring lasteth not alway,
Soon comes on the Winter day,

Blasting all the flowers we bring—
Blighting all the hopes of Spring.

Life is like the shady stream
   That joyous wanders on,—
Like a poet's waking dream,
Which with flitting fancies teem,
   To build his hopes upon,—
'Til the tide comes, swift and strong,
Filling up with Truth and Wrong,
'Til at last its waters pour,
Mingling with the ocean's roar.

THEBAZILE.

"And in that land, oh, is it not sweet
To know that the mother and child will meet!"

IT was in the month of September—
  The gloomiest month of the year—
When the Summer is loath to parting,
  Ere the leaves grow yellow and sere;—
A month of dark sadness and sorrow,
  Joy dawneth still over its gloom,
Tho' through all its weeping and watching,
  It hath brought but the cradle and tomb.

The day was hot and oppressive—
  I sighed for the cooling shade;
I saunter'd forth to the wood-land,
  Where gently the South breeze play'd—
In a darken'd and dim old forest,
  By the banks of a rushing stream—
And I laid me down and muséd
  O'er a poet's waking dream.

And the thought of days departed
   Rushed over my weary soul,
An ease for its sorrow and pining—
   Then upward the vista did roll;
I knelt by the side of my mother,
   In the shades of the dusky even,
And she bade me pray to our Father
   Who dwelleth in yonder Heaven;

She taught me the love of a Saviour,
   Who came to this world of ours
And offered Himself as a ransom—
   'T was like dew on the blushing flowers;
Thus, every evening and morning,
   As I humbly knelt by her side,
She taught me of God, and of Jesus
   Who for sinners as I had died;

She told me, when here He had wander'd—
   Folding me close to her breast,—
That mothers oft brought Him their children,
   Whom He took on his knee and blessed;
Her lessons of sweet instruction
   I remember in later years,
And the hopes of my early childhood
   Loom up through its sorrows and tears.

But Time came on with his changes,
   And her brow grew marble-like pale—
Her eyes were darken'd and sunken—
   Their lustre forever had failed;
Her hands they were blue-cold and icy—
   Her loved voice was silenc'd fore'er;—
The lips were now mute that had taught me
   My morning and evening prayer.

It was a bright morn in September—
   Tho' a sadden'd and lone one to me—
I was brought to the home of my mother,
   The bride of Death's angel to see;—
So I know that the flowers in Autumn
   All wither at the breath of the blast,
Ere the snows of the coming Winter
   A blight o'er their being cast.

It was a bright morn in September—
   Ten Summers have flown since then,
And over their pathways the roses
   Have faded and blossom'd again;
Yet still through earth's dreariest mazes,
   'Midst its cares, its pleasures, and fears,
I behold the same smile of my mother
   That she bore in my earlier years.

Oh! heavy the grief and the sorrow
  That saw her consigned to the tomb;
But Faith pointed up to yon Heaven,
  And Hope bade me cheer in my gloom;
I well knew that up thro' the ether
  Her spirit rejoicing had gone,
To dwell with the Father Eternal,
  From the realms of mortality flown.

Through the years of beauty and sunshine
  That have gone to the past since then,
There hover'd e'er by me an angel
  Unseen by the visions of men;
In the lovely bright flowers of Summer
  I behold the light of her smile,
And all through the bleak days of Winter
  Her face beameth on me the while.

I remember one evening in Autumn,
  When my mind was laden'd with care,
To my ears came the voice of my mother,
  And childhood's loved spirit of prayer;
I knelt on the green sward beside me,
  To my Father I lifted my soul,
And ere I had risen the waters
  Of peace o'er my troubles had roll'd.

It was in the ides of September—
   The gloomiest month of the year,
When the leaves are tinged with crimson,
   And the meadows grow brown and sere ;—
A month of dark sadness and sorrow,
   Yet joy dawneth over its gloom,
Tho' through all its weeping and watching,
   It hath brought but the cradle and tomb.

THE DYING TRADER.

Out upon the boundless prairies, as the evening shadows fell,
Chimed the close of Sabbath holy from the Mission chapel-bell,
And the soothing breezes gambol'd 'mong the dewy-laden flowers
Which the golden sunlight kissed the long bright Summer hours.

Upon a wigwam's bed of fur a pale-face dying lay,—
His companion watched beside him thro' the weary restless day;
They were traders from the valleys of the Quaker Land of Penn,
And had left their homes and kindred for the haunts of savage
 ·men.

Slowly passed the hour of midnight—dimmer grew the lamp of
 life ;
Its cares were almost ended—ceased its agony and strife,

But flickering yet and fitful glimmered still the fading light,
As the candle in the socket brightens in the gloom of night.

It was nigh the morning hour, for the fire was burning low,
And Allie lifted up his head—life's tide was ebbing slow;—
Then unto his lone companion—though the lamp was growing
    dim—
With a smile upon his features—he spoke to comfort him.

      Come up nearer, closer, brother,
        There is something I would say,
      For my voice is growing feebler,
        And I know I'll pass to-day;
      Come up nearer, closer, brother,
        And I'll whisper in your ear
      Messages for far-off kindred
        When I'm no longer here.

      Tell my father, when you see him,
        To think kindly of his son,
      To forgive his boyish waywardness,
        And pardon what he'd done;
      Tell him the counsels which he gave
        Have never been forgot;
      That I ever bore his words in mind
        Whate'er had been my lot.

Tell him I died repentant
  For the many sins of yore;
That I'll meet him on the portals
  Of the great eternal shore:
In that distant land I'll wait him—
  In those regions of the blest,
"Where the wicked cease from troubling
  And the weary are at rest."

Tell my mother not to weep for me,
  Her eldest and her pride,
For she's another boy at home—
  There's Willie by her side;
Tell her I e'er rememberéd
  The lessons which she taught,
And all her words of purity
  With love and kindness fraught;

For ever in the even
  And the morning of the day,
She drew me nigh unto her knee
  And taught me how to pray;
I remember yet when first
  Unto her side I came,
Then she told me of a God
  And a blessed Redeemer's name.

Tell sister Alice, when I'm gone,
　To remember what I said
When I bade her last "good-bye"—
　And think kindly of the dead;
I know she'll miss me often
　As the evening shadows fall,
But I'll never see her dear-loved face,
　Nor hear her sweetly call.

Tell her, her words of solace
　Were as dew unto the flowers;
They reviv'd this fainting heart of mine
　In sorrow's darkest hours;
O, deathless is a sister's love!
　For she took me by the hand
And paved a golden pathway up
　Unto the "better land."

Tell Will to never be so wild
　As his erring brother's been—
To shun the paths that lead to vice,
　The tempter's snare, and sin;
Nor leave the humble cottage home,
　As his wayward brother's done;
But should comfort sister Alice
　When I have passed and gone.

Give him the precious book which lies
   Beneath my resting head;
I know he'll ever cherish it
   In remembrance of the dead;
Tell him to study deeply
   Its words of living truth,
'T will be a strong support in age—
   A morning star in youth.

A word for our loved pastor—
   O, blessings on his head,
And blessings on his kindly voice,
   When I am with the dead;
God bless him in his labors,
   And when his task is done
I will meet him on the confines
   Of the land beyond the sun.

There yet is one—I'd ne'er forgot—
   A loving heart to mine,
As faithful as the ivy-vines
   That around the oak entwine;—
But softly, oh I warn you,
   Oh, slowly to her speak,
Lest the silver chain may loose
   And the golden bowl may break.

Tell her never to repine,
    Or weep for him who 's gone,
But be hopeful still and faithful,
    And wander fearless on ;
I know that sorrow's threads will weave
    With the life-woof of her day,
Yet there 's One above, oh, tell her,
    Who 'll soothe her on her way.

Farewell, farewell once more,
    For my eyes are growing dim,
And ere many moments longer
    My soul will be with Him;
Soon shall cease this heart's low throbbings—
    Soon life's weary strife be o'er;—
Oh, live so that you may meet me
    When " time shall be no more !"

But, O, I 'm growing weaker—
    Death's film o'erclouds mine eyes—
Yet a bright and holy light
    Gleameth down from Paradise !
O ! softly raise me up,—
    There are sweet sounds on the air ;—
Do n't you hear the seraphs calling?—
    You will meet—will meet me *there !*

As fades the radiant star-light before the splendor of the day,
So went out the life of Allie — so meekly passed away,
And the pure light of the morning shown upon a pallid face,
Which yester-dawn had brighten'd with almost angelic grace.

His comrade, on the 'morrow, saw him lowered in the grave,
Where the Yellowstone's bright waters the far Western prairies
      lave;
There he calmly rests in slumber in his lowly narrow bed,
With the deep tread of the red-man echoing dull above his head.

CARRIE.

"She hath laid her down by the crystal river,
To bathe in its waters of life forever."

We have lain the bud of our promise down
  To rest in the darksome mold,
For the light within had flicker'd and flown—
  And the pure warm heart was cold.

Now the crisping snow lies above her head,
  And low is the wind's chill moan
That ruffles the sheet on her lowly bed—
  But the spirit afar hath flown.

The glorious dawn of immortal life
  Gilds the hope of our joy above,
And the heavy grief of this bitter strife
  Is sunk in the light of His love.

With a golden harp in her little hand—
  An emerald crown on her brow—
She treadeth the halls of the "better land,"
  And chanteth a sweet strain now.

HOUSEHOLD JEWELS.

"Some like angel-whispers passed away from earth,
With its lights and shadows, aud its death and birth—
Gone are lovesome voices, gone its kindly mirth,
Empty chairs are standing round the old-time hearth."—ELLEN LOUISE.

OUR EMILY.

OH! how we loved her gentle name,
  So innocent and dear,
But now there's sadness in the sound,
  That makes us shrink with fear;
We'll never hear that voice again,
  Which rang so loud and free,
For death hath hushed the merry laugh
  Of our dear Emily!

Her voice of glee we'll hear no more,
  Nor see her tripping by;
There's silence in our home to-night—
  Death's angel hath been nigh;

Her loving eyes are closed and dim,
   Their light we ne'er shall see—
Oh! she has sunk to her dreamless sleep—
   Our loving Emily!

Within the grave-yard's silent gloom,
   Near by the elm tree's shade,
Where the harvest moon looks cheerless down,
   Our darling's lowly laid;
And there she 'll rest forever and aye,
   Unto eternity;
The pride of our hearth is far away—
   Heaven's angel, Emily!

OUR LIZZIE.

ANOTHER of our household band
  Hath wander'd from our side;
She with the gentle eye of blue—
  The rosy cheek—hath died,
And in the grave, cold, damp, and dim,
  Our Lizzie lonely lies;
The death-frost nipped our bursting bud
  To blossom in Paradise.

The glimm'ring spark of our household lamp
  Hath flicker'd and died away,—
The loveliest and brightest hopes
  Of earth seem loath to stay;
And she hath gone to Heaven to meet
  Our love-lost Emily,—
Those golden climes—those happy shores
  Of Immortality.

We know our darling Lizzie 's gone
  To that bright home in the skies,
Where never-ending praises sound
  And eternal incense rise;
To our Father's house our Lizzie went
  To the mansions far away,
Where over her brow shall ever gleam
  The light of ineffable day!

OUR WILLIE.

WE have a darling still at home,
  A gentle, loving boy;
No grief hangs low'ring o'er his brow,
  Nor darkness o'er his joy;
His eye of black is ever by,
  His form is ever near;
His merry voice is full of glee—
  Our household's only cheer.

Oh! when our wo was keen and sore,
  And the loved death-hush'd and chill,—
We knew our Father had taken them,
  Nor repin'd we at His will;
But in our grief we thanked Him much—
  A form yet by us came—
A loving, winsome boy he is,
  And Willie is his name.

10

Oh! Father, spare our boy to us,
   It 't is Thy gracious will,
And o'er his pathway hover close,
   And keep him from all ill;
But oh, if him Thou yet shouldst call
   To where our loved have gone—
Our Lizzie and our Emily—
   May our trust in Thee be strong.

OUR BIRD.

ANOTHER bird hath nestled close
   Among our household band—
A bird, I ween, from Paradise,
   Given by our Father's hand;
We thank Thee, Father for Thy gift—
   This gift of holy love—
Oh, make it meet on earth below
   To live with Thee above!

A blessing of priceless value—
   A jewel rich and rare—
A boon from Heav'n, but far more fit
   To bud and blossom there;
Oh, Father save it from the scorn
   And temptings of this world;
And may Thy Word be its delight—
   Its truths to it unfurl'd!

Oh! teach us so to nourish it—
    To bring it up for Thee,
That when it leaves this world of ours,
    Thy glory it may see!
With Willie and our Bird at home,
    Our griefs are hushed amain;
For the vacant seats of our lone hearth
    Are all filled up again!

SWEET SPRING IS HERE.

The fairies from the South-Land
    Have been romping o'er our hills,
And set to gentle music
    The little babbling rills,—
Have scattered richest jewels
    O'er valley and o'er lea—
Loved " darlings of the forest"
    Blooming in the wilds, Annie.

The maple 's dyed with crimson,
    And the spice-wood 's crowned with gold ;
The hawthorn 's white with blossoms,
    And the violets gem the wold,—
Bright glowing buds of beauty,
    And streams of melody,
Enliveneth the Spring-time,
    And rejoiceth all, Annie.

Oh, long the dreary Winter
    Paled the soften'd brow of Spring !
My heart had longed for flowers,
    And for birds of brightened wing
To thrill me with their music,
    And to charm me with their glee ;—
But *now* the May is dawning,
    And the Spring-time 's here, Annie.

The Southern breeze is wafting
    Fragrance from the isles away,
And dews of even sparkle
    In the fair, young flowers of May ;
How sweet 's the breath of roses
    From the sunny far South sea,
That 's borne by gentlest zephyrs
    To our Northern home, Annie.

How gloriously the sunlight
    Gilds the blushing cheeks of morn,
And dew-drops gleaming, glitter
    In the flowers they adorn ;
My soul leaps up with gladness,
    In its wildness and its glee,
And I thank the One above us
    For his kindness e'er, Annie.

How radiant is the noon-light
   Glinting down upon the streams,
As golden halls do glisten
   In the pleasant Land of Dreams ;
The glare of Summer's mid-day
   Brings a fevered brow for me ;
The noon-tide of the Spring time
   Driveth far all care, Annie.

How glorious is the eve-light
   Fading in the distant West,
As the king of day departeth
   To his weary couch of rest,
Yet ever leaves behind him
   Halos golden bright for me—
How sweet 's a spring-time even
   In our Northern home, Annie !

But Spring-time lasts not ever,
   With its buds and with its flowers,
With birds all gaily singing
   In the pleasant wild-wood bowers,
For Summer and the Autumn
   Soon will follow in *its* glee,
And icy, dreary Winter
   Then will dawn o'er all, Annie.

O, the fairies from the South-land
   Have been romping o'er our hills,
And set to sweetest music
   The little babbling rills,—
Have scatter'd richest jewels
   O'er valley and o'er lea—
Loved darlings of the Spring-time
   Blooming in the wilds, Annie.

THE FIRST SWEET ROSE OF JUNE.

ON the whiten'd walls of the homestead,
   Facing the Southern clime,
Bloometh early in June sweet roses—
   The first of the Summer-time;
And the one I have culled this even
   Is fresh from the parent tree,
Where it blew in the dewy morning,
   So gorgeous and fair, Nellie!

O, the blast of the lingering Winter
   Ne'er came on the kiss of the Spring,
To pale the flush of the roses;
   And the birds of golden wing
Sang even and morn 'mong the leaflets
   So sweetly wild and free,
Till their little throats thrilled with music
   To the joy of the flowers, Nellie!

11

The breath of the South-land breezes
   Awaketh the buds to life,
So the songs of " My Loved Ideal"
   With sweets untold are rife,
And my heart is filled with emotion,
   As playing by in her glee,
She steals from my brow, care-wearied,
   A kiss, then fleeth, Nellie!

How I love, in the glorious even,
   To gather sweet flowers and rare,
And twine for " My Loved Ideal"
   Wreaths for her braided hair,—
Wreaths of the young June roses,
   Bright for her melody,
And love for the unheard music
   She keepeth for me, Nellie!

Think not 'tis the maiden Fancy,
   With whom I often do rove
And wander on airy pinions
   Through many a sun-lit grove—
That ever enchants my vision,—
   A sister to *her* she'll be,—
'T is my heart-love and Ideal,
   —Know you her not, Nellie?

Soon, soon, alas ! will the leaflets
    Wither and fade away ;
Thus ever the dear June roses
    'Neath the glare of the Summer day ;
Soon, soon, the bright buds of beauty
    From the smiles of earth will flee,
And the breath and balm of·flowers
    Will be wafted no more, Nellie !

They 're a type that *all* is fleeting,
    That soon all must pass away ;
As the gems of the radiant Summer,
    So man in the dust must lay ;
Yes, I and " My Loved Ideal,"
    With her golden melody,
Must pass away with earth's weary
    To the unknown climes, Nellie !

LITTLE ELLEE G.

THERE are meek eyes softly beaming
    With a pure and holy light,
As the first eve-star that trembles
    On the corridors of night;
And within their hallowed cloisters
    Lies a soul of melody—
Soft blue eyes of tender meaning
    Hath dear little Ellee G.

There's a seeming sadness resting
    On that pale smooth brow of thine,
Yet a radiant beauty gloweth
    Out upon this life of mine;
Now the sunshine purely glistens
    On thy brow and in thine e'e,—
May life's shadows darken never
    O'er thee, darling Ellee G.

There is golden music, darling,
    In thy half-lisped baby-words,
And as sweet as morning matins
    Of the joyous Summer birds;
O, I love thy merry prattle,
    And withal thy childish glee,—
Dear to me, indeed 's the life-tones,
    Darling little Ellee G.

Blessings on thee, darling Ellee,
    Heaven's blessings on thee rest,
He 'll safe guide thee thro' life's voyage,
    Whom you say you love the best—
Safely guard thee thro' the tempest,
    O'er the stormy wild strife-sea—
Watch thee thro' the gloomy shadows—
    Dear-loved darling Ellee G.

THE PRAIRIE FLOWER.

TO A. W. D., OF GARNAVILLO, IOWA.

THERE's a flower that blooms in the Western wold,
　　Far away from our forests stark,
For it fades and dies when transplanted afar
　　In our wild-woods dim and dark;
And blushing it lives in its Western home,
　　Where anon at the twilight hour
It folds its snowy petals to sleep—
　　The lovely Prairie Flower.

In the Summer eve how I long to be
　　Far out on the Prairies wild,
And pluck the rich gems as I wander'd o'er,
　　A merry-hearted child,—
To watch them then as they blush'd at the kiss
　　Of the ev'ning's dewy shower;—
O, dear to my heart in this Eastern clime,
　　Is the Western Prairie Flower!

The sun on the Western wave may set,
  The mid-summer days may flee,
The chilling breath of the Autumn may come,
  Or the blast from the Arctic sea—
Yet bloometh as ever, 'mid sunlight or shade,
  Tho' blighting may be the hour—
As fair thro' the Winter as Summer's bright day—
  The gorgeous Prairie Flower!

Oh! give me the love for which I have yearned—
  A treasure I'll ever hold dear,
A heart which will whisper its love unto mine,
  Ne'er to fail in Adversity's year;—
Tho' Fortune may frown (its friendship's ne'er true),
  And care come with its dark power,
Oh, give me a friend that will ever remain
  As true as the Prairie Flower!

THERE'S A HOME IN HEAVEN.

WHEN your heart is earth-weary, and you long for a spot
Where strife never comes and grief is forgot—
Where the care of this world ne'er intrudes on its rest—
Turn your thoughts toward Heaven—the Home of the Blest!

There far, far away, where the sunlight doth fall,
Never dimming its glow on the gold-jewel'd wall,—
Where the sorrows of earth in their blight never come,
In the loved Spirit-Land—there, there is that Home.

Where the sweet music echoes throughout the fair skies,
And the anthems of praises eternally rise ;—
There the heart-stricken dove at last will find rest,
In those regions of Light—the Land of the Blest;

When the toiling hath hushed, and the heavenly calm
That soothes the lone heart, as the sweet-chanted psalm
Floateth softly away far o'er the bright plain,
Where the Love of ineffable glory doth reign.

The light which pervadeth the lov'd Paradise
Is holier far than e'er seen 'neath the skies;
There the stars shimmer bright o'er valley and lea—
In that Home far away—Heaven's " sunnie countrie."

Oh, hope for no place on life's trackless path,
Free from its temptations, its wiles, and its wrath ;
'T is the lot of earth mortals to tarry awhile,
To be lured by its snares and deceived by its smile.

Oh, why then repine, for not in this world
Is a spot where the Banner of Peace was ne'er furl'd,—
Where the joyness of life hath never been riven,—
Look behind the dim portal—there 's no Home but Heaven !

Be trusting and faithful ! Hope ever in God—
He will not forsake you 'neath life's weighty load ;
'T is ever earth's weary alone long for rest—
Beyond the dark valley is the Home of the Blest !

12

KOSSUTH AND HUNGARY!

FROM o'er the mighty ocean—the roaring waste of blue—
Comes freedom's greatest champion, the firmly tried and true.
He is with us—he has landed safely on our shores from far:
The despot's fear, the tyrant's hate—the noble, brave Magyar!

O, leader of the people! O, freedom's exiled son!
O, Kossuth, great and glorious! Hungaria's Washington!
We give thee our heart's best welcome, to our firesides and our
    homes—
From the oppression of the tyrants on the Austro-Russian
    thrones!

We welcome thee, O chieftain, from Europe's classic land!
Lo! a brighter day is dawning, when shall fail the tyrant's hand;
When the mighty shout of FREEDOM shall arise from Europe's
    hills,
And the deep and rushing rivers breathe the fervor from the rills;

When Despotism's rule of iron shall awe no more the world,
When haughty kings, tho' sceptred, from their glittering thrones
    be hurled :
And the light of FREEDOM blazon, wherever man is found,
To nerve his soul to action and strike the tyrants down ?

O, Hungary ! brave Hungary ! ere now thou hadst been free,
But the base-born traitors sold thee to the beck of Tyranny !
The barbaric Austro-Tyrant called the Despot to his aid,
And thy bright hopes of the future low in the dust were laid !

Thou 'rt fallen now, but not forc'er—the day is hast'ning on,
When thy people, all united, shall hurl the tyrant down,
And the galling chains of slavery shall be asunder torn ;
When oppression's hour of darkness ushers in the golden morn !

We watch the coming contest, for the clouds grow black amain,
That settle over Europe's hills and on each fertile plain ;
GOD be with the noble patriots who no more will bend the knee
To a tyrant, crown'd and sceptred, but have vowed THEY WILL BE
    FREE !

Ay, welcome, chief illustrious, to Liberty's own land !
Thrice welcome gallant leader of Europa's Freedom band !
We welcome thee, with out-stretch'd arms, from o'er the surging sea,
Countless blessings on thee, brave Magyar ! Friend of Truth and
    Liberty !

WHEN I DIE.

WHEN I die, oh dearest Clarence, and the death-film shades my
    eye,—
When this mortal frame, so weary, putteth off mortality,
And you bear me from the homestead, from your sight forever-
    more,
Take me to the quiet valley, by my own lov'd river's shore.

Where the lichens grow the thickest, and the maple stately tow'rs,
And the grove is filled with sweetness from the dewy-laden'd
    flow'rs;
Where I can list the roaring, in the balmy even-tide,
Of my own, my native streamlet;—you will lay me by its side.

Let not the hollow gray-stone above me ever rest;
I would rather have the cold damp sod lay on my peaceful breast;
Let the pale flow'rs of mother earth alone breathe forth my
    name,—
I wish not a polish'd marble, as a herald vaunting fame.

A few short years must pass away, and we 'll be forgotten still—
I care not for men's scorn or praise, if I but do His will,—
Oh, often for the Unattained, unsatisfied below,
I pray'd to fly, ere many days, where my spirit longed to go.

But I shall wait His 'biding time, when He shall think it best,
To call my spirit away from earth and fold me to His breast,
And in the light of His smile I 'll bask, rejoicing in its ray,
Forever and forever, in one eternal day.

All through the darken'd valley He will take me by the hand,—
Lead me safely to the portals of that bright and happy land;
—The glory of His righteousness ne'er dimmeth on its shore,
And myriad hosts of angels harp His praises and adore.

Oh, I would have you when I die plant flow'rs upon my grave,
In the quiet, lonely valley, by the river's sparkling wave;
Plant the willow at the foot, and the fir-tree at the head,
It will soften all your grief, when you come to see the dead.

In the calm eve of Summer, when the earth is hush'd and still,
You will come, my dearest Clarence—come and hear the robins
    trill,
As they warble in the thicket, or are nodding in the glen ;—
When the flowers, too, are sleeping, you will come and see me
    then.

When the starry hosts of heaven their unwearied vigils keep—
When earth is wrapped in silence, and the shadows groweth
  deep—
When the gem on Heaven's coronal shines from the dazzling
  height,
You will come and see my grave in the gorgeousness of night.

Good night now, dearest Clarence, for the sun hath gone to
  rest,—
Oh, calm it sunk to sleep upon the ocean's heaving breast;
Good night! my eyes are heavy, and my sight is growing dim,—
Oh, remember what I told you, when I go home to Him!

WHEN I WOULD DIE.

In the softened Summer's twilight
  May my spirit take its wing,
When all is hushed to quiet,
  Then to hear the angels sing,
As through th' unclouded ether
  Gently, low, my name they'd call—
As the shadows groweth deeper
  On the painted cottage wall ;—

Ere the lovely sweet June roses
  Cease their blow upon the lea,
Would I wish the kind Death-angel,
  With his message come to me ;
Oh, there 's something in the stillness
  Of a genial Summer eve,
When o'er all 's a golden beauty—
  Then for rest my soul doth grieve.

In the hallow'd Summer even,
   When the fading daylight dies,
Would I wish to leave earth's sorrows
   For the glorious golden skies;
Where the never ending pæan
   On the perfum'd air is borne,
And the shimmering sunlight glitters
   O'er Heaven's eternal morn.

But be it eve or morning,
   It matters not to me
When shall come old Death, the Reaper,
   His harvest wide to see;—
Oh, may we all be ready
   To cross unto that shore,
There, with angels, swell the chorus,
   And the Holy One adore.

"OUR WILLIE, TOO, HATH GONE!"

" The beautiful Virgin Mother,
  Down bending her low from the skies,
Wove a glory around his forehead,
  And folded the lids o'er his eyes."—ELLEN LOUISE.

FROM our hearth-stone bright, the sunshine 's gone,
  And sorrow alone sits by;
Grief-stricken we gaze on the vacant chair—
  The angel of Death 's been nigh,
And snatched from our side our cherish'd boy,
  And paléd that noble brow;—
His eyes are closed in their last, long sleep,
  For the mold grows over them now.

The merry laugh and the cheerful voice
  Are heard no more in the hall,
For gone fore'er is our Willie dear—
  He heedeth no more our call;
Far, far away with the spirit-band,
  His gentle voice is heard,
Echoing through the celestial land,
  Like the strains of a bright-winged bird.

13

Like the Summer flowers in Autumn-time
   Fade at the Polar breath,
So sunk to rest our cherub-boy
   In the icy arms of Death ;
Yet as the genial Spring again
   The birds and flowers renew,
So will Heaven's eternal Spring
   Revive our Willie, too !

Tho' we on earth may sorrow on,
   And sundered be earthly ties,
Still we hope to meet our darling boy
   In the realms of Paradise—
Where the golden crown on his marble brow
   Presses light on his sunny hair,
And gorgeous gleameth the light of God
   O'er the angel spirit there.

THE DYING BOY TO HIS SISTER.

WILL the happy Spring come soon,
   Or be long ere Summer 's here—
And the roses sweet of June,
   Golden month of all the year?
Tell me, tell me, sister mine,
   Will I see the flowers more,
Will I rove again along
   Our own-loved river's shore?

Will I hear the warbling birds
   Swell their matins o'er the lea,
Will they, in the Summer eve,
   Sing a plaintive strain for me?
Tell me, truly, sister dear,
   Will I see again the wild,
Where we loved so well to play
   In the day-close hushed and mild?

When around my flowing hair,
    Brightest flowers your hand entwined,
As our wearied brows were fanu'd
    By the soft and cool South wind?
When the blossoms on the hawthorn,
    In their blow I culled for you?—
Oh, how loved those days of sunshine
    Which the early Summer knew.

Will I never, never see
    Those gleesome days again?
Oh, tell me, is this Death!—
    Is my longing all in vain?
Ah, yes, sweet sister dear,
    I will never see them more,
For ere another sun shall set
    Life's day-dreams will be o'er.

ANNIE.

Oh, she was young, and beautiful, and fair,
　　And ne'er a care had shadow'd o'er her brow;
With sunshine playing with her golden hair,
　　Deep in the vista's sheen, I see her now.

She was a pure, a bright and artless child,
　　Who loved to sit aside her mother's knee,
And looking in her face so calm and mild,
　　Sing some sweet gushing strain of melody.

Her looks, I know were all of tenderness and truth;
　　Her gentle heart had never, never known,
The bitter pangs of after life, for youth
　　Had never brought the world's more callous frown.

I saw her last one genial Summer's eve;
   The dew was kissing all the weary flowers—
When sighing zephyrs for the sun-light grieve,
   And sing a mournful strain thro' twilight hours.

Her head was resting on her mother's breast,
   Her calm eyes fixed their purely light above;
And as the stars at dawn, she sunk to rest
   Relying on the promise of His love.

The stars looked dim and pale when Annie went,
   The moon was sad—it never smiled since then—
And low in grief our weary heads were bent,
   We knew we'd never see her *here* again.

We laid her by the stream she loved so well,—
   There calmly rests she in her home of clay,—
Her spirit in Our Father's house doth dwell
   Whose gold-light with her sunny tresses play..

A CHILD AFAR TO HIS MOTHER.

TO MRS. M. R. H., OF MEMPHIS, TENNESSEE.

FROM the sunny meads of South-land—
   From its vines and orange flowers,
And the voice of sweet birds singing
   Gaily in its wilding bowers,—
Where the radiant sunlight shimmers
   Over rills of melody,
Lightly dancing on its waters,
   As they ripple to the sea ;

Where the smile of Spring-time ever
   Gladdeneth each pleasant face—
And the golden brow of beauty
   Her way of sheen doth trace ;—
To my distant haunts of childhood,
   To my mother kind and mild,
Wings the warm and heartfelt message
   From her wand'ring, lonely child.

O'er the threshold oft Death's angel
  Hath crossed with wo and gloom;
At last he hath ta'en my sister,
  Whom we laid in the cheerless tomb;
Oh, she was loving, and gentle,
  With the tresses light o'er her brow,
And a look that would shadow an angel's—
  Her spirit is with me now.

Oh, a light went out in the homestead,
  With its halo all golden and bright,
Yet the ray-star that liveth undying,
  Is lighting my soul to-night:
Though the glow of a Summer even
  May bring her no more to me,
Still up in the house of Our Father,
  Again my sister I'll see.

I pine and long for the North-land,
  Though the South-clime vales are dear,
For I see not the smile of my mother,
  And my home can never be here:
Oh, the love of a mother's holier
  Than aught to be found upon earth,
And the bands of affection ne'er loosen
  That encircle the homestead hearth.

Away, where the Father of Rivers
    Rushes on with its darkly tide,
There riseth the walls of the homestead—
    A mother dwells by its side;
Far, far away from thee, mother,
    Thy only child doth roam,
Broad lands, and mounts, and rivers
    Lie between him and his home.

I yearn for the days of Summer,
    When joyful I 'll come to thee,
For I'm weary all day of this South-land;
    I long for thy smile to see;
I 'll hasten far, far, to the North-land,
    To see thee, oh mother dear,
To feel on my brow thy kisses—
    For home can never be here.

I send thee an off'ring all holy,
    Of tenderness deep, and truth;
Thou who hast watched o'er my childhood,
    And guided my wayward youth;
I 'll come, when the glow of the Summer
    Shall fever my care-worn brow:
Oh would that the bliss of thy presence—
    My mother, were with me now,

DARLING LIZZIE.

"With their harps in their hands, they have beckoned her **home**,
To the bosoms of loved ones that before them have gone;
She has heeded their call, and has joined them above,
To dwell with them ever in glory and love."—NELLIE G.

THE halo around us has vanished—
　　The light from our hearth has gone,
And the Angel of Grief sits by us,
　　Weeping—oh, sad and lone—
For our darling and our loved one
　　Has wandered away from our side;
As the flowers of Spring oft chilleth,
　　So Lizzie, our all hath died!

Oh! the Death-Angel came with his pinions,
　　Folding her to his breast,
And the waft of his breath was blighting;
　　Softly she sunk to her rest:

And her cheeks grew pale and hueless,
  For the rosy flush was fled ;
We laid her away in her beauty,
  By the side of the " early dead."

Oh, the blast of sin and sorrow
  Ne'er came with their chill embrace,
Nor the wo of life, or its trials,
  Ne'er shaded her innocent face ;—
Far, far away 'bove the ether,
  'Neath the blush of the jewel'd skies,
Is the light of our home-hearth singing
  Heaven's glorious melodies.

Up, up to the House of Our Father—
  Up, up to the Holy One's throne,
Where the sun-light ever gleameth,
  Our Lizzie—our all has gone ;
She waiteth there our coming,
  When the trials of life are o'er ;
Then why pine we here in sorrow,
  " She 's not lost—but gone before."

MY HEART'S WHISPER.

FROM A POEM ADDRESSED TO ————————.

————————"But all my days
Walk with still footsteps and with humble eyes,
An everlasting hymn within my soul."

LIFE is growing fainter, shorter,
   And I hear one at the door,—
Yes, I see the grim Death Angel
   Standing on the solemn shore;
But my heart sinks not within me,
   For a kind and gracious hand
Will support me thro' the river
   That divides us from that land.

What's the world's cold frown, which often
   Fills our cup of sorrow here?—
What are all the wearyings restless,
   If our Saviour still is near:
"Father! at thy throne, this midnight,
   Unto Thee, my pray'rs ascend,
I would crave, thro' life, thy blessing,
   Till its journey here shall end.

Teach my wayward spirit, Father,
　Ne'er to murmur at thy will,—
Ne'er to mind the world, how selfish—
　Nor repine its every ill;
May we trust in thy arm ever—
　Steadfast in thy faith e'er prove,
And remem'bring 't is far better
　Thee to serve, oh God of love?"

—What care we for poor earth's baubles?
　Soon they all must pass away;
What for all life's gilded trappings?
　It, in truth, is but a day;
May our thoughts to HIM e'er wander,
　As our way we tread below,
Ne'er forgetting that all mercy
　From our Father's hand doth flow.

When upon us comes the tempest,
　Fearless may we meet our doom;
Keeping watch toward the beacon
　Which shall guide us safely home:
All our hopes we 'll rest in Jesus—
　He will all our fears remove;
O! the day will soon be dawning
　When we both will meet above.

STANZAS.

The night is cold and cheerless,
  And on the crisping snow,
The star-light, dim and shrouded,
  Lies heavy, dull, and low :
Alone, I sit in musing
  O'er what the Past hath brought,
Yet mindful of the Present—
  What with the Future fraught.

Across my mind there cometh
  A form I love so dear—
Of one oft viewed in Dream-land,
  And in the Real near—
A loving heart and kindred—
  Oh, kisses for his brow !
I would that he were with me,
  I'd have him by me now.

I love that look so gentle—
  That sparkling eye and bright;
Their expression soft and tender,
  Their holy mellow light—
The radiance of that spirit
  I feel upon my heart;
Oh, never may its halo
  From the shrined cells depart.

A love all pure and holy,
  All tenderness and truth,
Is borne for the companion,
  Of trusting early youth;
With him I'm e'er contented—
  Oh, gracious boon of love!
A friendship true as ours
  Must sure endure above!

I would that I were like him;
  So patient, kind, and mild!
Still I try to do my duty,
  An erring, wayward child:
I know he strives to follow
  The paths the Saviour trod—
And I say as Ruth to Naomi,
  " *Thy* God shall be my God!"

In morning, noon, and even,
   Whene'er I kneel in prayer,
In fervent supplication,
   His name is mentioned there;
Oh, on his head rest blessings
   From Thrones of Grace above;
May joys untold await him—
   My Life—my Light—my Love!

But life is short and fleeting,
   And Death may come to-day—
Deep in our cup fill sorrow,
   And part us on our way:
Yet may we meet in Heaven
   When time shall be no more,
And chime our songs of praises
   With the angelic choir.

THOU 'RT NOT ALONE.

"I am alone! there is no breast
Doth pant lu unison with mine."—[J. F. WEISHAMPEL, JR.

THOU 'RT not alone! for there's a breast
Doth pant in unison with thine—
A voyager on life's gloomy sea—
A friend in truth—thou 'rt not unknown!
And soon will come that peaceful rest,
As for this weary soul of mine;
Then cast off care, and be thou free—
That cankers life—thou 'rt not alone.

Though thou 'rt a piece of "drift" that 's tossed
With wildness on the desert shore,
Yet there is one afar from thee
Who treasures what away is thrown;
A traveler, too;—but oh, not lost,
For thou shalt sing forevermore;
Oh, if thou 'lt brave life cheerfully,
Thou wouldst not, shouldst not be alone.

Though o'er the vales the deer may play,
  And birds, and beasts in all their joy,
    May wildly, madly rove in glee,
      Why then should thy heart be cast down ;
Away with misery, away ;
  I call thee, come—though but a boy,
    A friend, indeed, with spirits free—
      With me thou couldst not be alone.

Oh, do not thus one moment stay ;
  Look up to Faith's bright, glorious beam ;
    Let Hope thy holiest guerdon be—
      And strike anew thy sweetest tone.
Weep not ;—O chase those tears away ;
  Soon mayst thou wear a heavenly gleam ;
    A friendly hand I give to thee,
      With me thou 'lt never be alone.

STANZAS.

TO W. D. B. ON HIS MARRIAGE.

I WELCOME thee back to thy boyhood's home,
   To thy native streamlet's tide ;
I welcome thee back to thy home again,
   With thy young and blooming bride.

With a heart-warm love for the " good old time,"
   With its joys, and smiles, and tears,—
And a ready hand, I welcome thee back,
   O, friend of my early years !

May sorrow ne'er rest on that brow of thine,
   Nor yet dim thy lady's e'e,
But with holy love be there ever nigh
   Peace and prosperity.

O, ye winds that blow over Time's stormy wave,
   Waft them gently o'er thy sea;
O, flowers of happiness bloom in their path,
   In joy or adversity.

Ay, I wish thee joy with thy cherished one,
   Dear friend of my boyhood's days,
Yes, I wish thee well, in thy manhood's prime,—
   Heaven watchful guard thy ways.

O, I welcome thee back to thy boyhood's home,
   The home of thy childhood's pride;
I welcome thee back to thy native hills,
   With thy young and blooming bride!

"I COME."

" And in his wild death-dreams
He yearned for HOME."—MS.

FATHER, I come !
    Thy spirit-voice afar I hear,
        Calling me home ;
    Sweet are the soft tones to my ear—
        Father, I come !

I come, I come !
    The ev'ning shades are dark'ning o'er
        Forest and dome ;
    All lonely seems the corridor—
        Father, I come !

Mother, I come !
    I hear thee calling hence thy child
        Unto his home,
    From out the night-heavens high and wild—
        Mother, I come !

I come ! I come
       For I have yearn'd since early day
          Afar to roam,
       And on thy breast my weary head to lay—
          Mother, I come !

Brother, I come !
       The Northern land 's been chill and drear
          Since thou art gone ;
       Still, still I pine in yearning here—
          Brother, I come !

Brother, I come !
       I fain would see thee ere I die
          Beneath our home ;
       O, can this be a fantasy—
          A dream ?—I come !

Sister, I come !
       To feel thy kiss upon my brow,
          My lov'd—my own !
       For grief hangs low'ring o'er me now—
          Sister, I come !

I come! I come!
    To hear thy gentle voice again,
      O cherished one!
    I'll love thee more and better, when
      I come! I come!

I come! I come!
    'T is but a dream—it cannot be!
      My descant's vain,—
    'T was a wild thought came over me,
      —Deceiv'd again.

O yes, I come!
    A light I see doth gleam afar.
      Within that home,
    Whose ev'ry radiant glow 's a star!
      I come! I come!

I come! I come!
    Up from my heart's deep chambers wells
      Yearnings for home,
    Where GOD in endless glory dwells,—
      I come! I come!

FATHER, I come !
    Up, up to streets of glist'ning gold,
      And em'rald dome ;
    Far, far away from earth, bleak, cold—
      FATHER, I come !

MY BOY-HOOD'S HOME.

" The sweet remembrance of the Past,—
Of scenes I hoped would longer last—
Thro' life will I retain."—K. W.

BRING back my boyhood's golden hours
  From the treasury of the past;—
Oh linger nigh ! life's first Spring flowers,
  That faded 'fore the blast;
The rocky cliff, the hill and glen,
  The joy and laughter free ;
I would I were a boy again—
  Oh bring them back to me.

Bring back my early childhood's home—
  The altar and the hearth,
The song of praise—devotion's tone—
  The lov'd that fled from earth ;
The days that flitted by so fast,
  —Life's streamlet to its sea,—
Which lie deep buried in the Past ;—
  Oh bring them back to me.

In Fancy's realms, I wander still
    By my boyhood's cherished home,
And gather flowers by brook or rill,
    And over woodlands roam ;
Oh linger nigh ! though visions dim
    And shadows faint ye be ;—
Tho' filled life's chalice to the brim,
    Yet bring them back to me !

TWO YEARS AGO.

Two long, long years have passed, to-day,
   Since near thy own White's wave,
Far from thy native home away,
   They made thy early grave ;
And oh, the sorrows deep that wrung
   This stricken heart of mine,
And darkened shadows o'er *me* hung
   Which never shall pall thine !

Oh, there is joyness 'round thee now,
   For grief doth never come
To blight the heart and shade the brow
   Within that glorious home ;
There's sun-light gleaming round thee there,
   And never cometh night,
For all is beautiful and fair
   Within that Home of Light.

I miss thee, Vincent, in the Spring,
　　When all are free and glad,
And though joy bids my spirit sing,
　　My lonely heart is sad;
Oh, childhood's days have passed away,
　　And thou hast wandered far,
Where never ends the golden day,
　　And every gem 's a star.

I miss thee in the Summer-time,
　　When flowers fill the dell,
When brooklets flow in silver rhyme,
　　And blows the lily-bell,
In bright July, or rosy June,
　　Or August's weary days,
In early dawn, or scorching noon,
　　Or even's peaceful haze.

I miss thee, Vincent, by the side
　　Of Susquehanna's stream,
Where oft we roved in gleeful pride,
　　Nor thought it *all* a dream,
Yet so it was; those days have pass'd,
　　And thou, my friend, hast gone,—
Too beautiful were they to last—
　　As shadows have they flown.

God grant that when this life shall close,
  And all its labor o'er,
Its trials and its direst woes
  To be felt nevermore,
That I may meet thee by the throne—
  The star-set throne above,
To help thee praise the Holy One,
  And sing His gracious love.

I WILL ALWAYS PRAY.

When the golden blush of morning
    Lighteth up the Eastern skies,
And the dew each flower adorning
    Sparkles like an angel's eyes;
When the day-god's rays are stealing
    O'er the eastern hills away,
Charming earth with their revealing,
    To my God I'll kneel I pray.

When the fervid glow of Summer,
    With its noon more sultry still,
And the zephyr's faint like murmur
    Sports along the gurgling rill;
When the flowrets droop and languish
    'Neath the scorching glare of day;
When my soul is fill'd with anguish,
    To my God I'll kneel and pray.

When the deep'ning shades of even
   Gather thick and dark o'er all ;
When the starry gems of Heaven,
   Gleaming thro' the sable pall,
True and holy vigils keeping
   O'er the kind departing day ;
While earth's weary ones are sleeping,
   To my God I'll kneel and pray !

L'ENVOI—TO ****.

THESE lays of mine, which I have gather'd here,
    Are but the out-bursts of an ardent heart,
    And of *thy* life and *mine* an earnest part,
For with their sweet inspirings came thy cheer
To soothe and bless me in my lonely hours,
    As a sweet joy-tide on life's restless sea;
    Yet in this wreath of humble minstrelsy
Thou may'st not find as sweetly fragrant flow'rs
As bards sublime have left to earth and fame,
    For these are simple, *heart-felt* lays of mine—
    Pure incense from its hallow'd inner shrine;
No meed of praise for them I ask or claim,
Save *thy* voice of approval; whate'er I 've done,
Are echoes caught from thee, O, dearest one!

CPSIA information can be obtained
at www.ICGtesting.com
Printed in the USA
LVHW031640281118
598533LV00023B/1066/P